Pretty Words. Nothing More.

An Unlikely Book of Poetry By
Andy Martello

This book is an original publication by Andy Martello and
Just A Martello Books.
Published by Andy Martello.

Cover design by Ty Hogan
Interior by Gretchen Shoemaker

"Naked" Edition: 2015
ISBN-13: 978-0692365571
ISBN: 0692365575

DEDICATION

To The RED Girls:
The Partner, The Secret, The Rescue,
The Passion, The Confidant,
AND
The Beautiful, Horrible Muse.

CONTENTS

ACKNOWLEDGMENTS

This book would not be possible without…

The patience and friendship of Ty Hogan, Gretchen
Shoemaker, Monica Walker Kodie,
Chelsea Crews, and Heather Perkins

The "You're a poet" encouragement of my brilliant editor,
Leslie Hoffman

The confusing, manipulative, and painful inspiration
provided by RED #5

Special thanks go to Just the Tip, located inside of
Whiskey Dick's bar in North Las Vegas, Nevada.
You've no idea how many poems were
written from within the kitchen.

FOREWORD

This book represents the first incarnation of *Pretty Words. Nothing More.* By design, it is stark, simple; with few frills and no images.

Those who have followed the evolution of this project through my Facebook pages know the original versions of these poems featured accompanying images to add to the experience and emotional impact. The deluxe edition of this book will feature brilliant original artwork and photographs from many supremely talented artists and photographers who were not only moved and inspired by the poems, but believed in the project enough to donate their own heartfelt work.

This book and the accompanying e-book are affordable products which will help fund the printing of the aforementioned deluxe edition, which will have high-quality images on glossy paper, a hard cover, a very limited print run, a new introduction, and additional poems. It is my sincere hope to bring a truly special book to the world that you will enjoy.

Since poetry is so personal and its worth is so subjective, having this "bare-bones" version allows the reader to focus specifically on the words and meaning behind them. I am very proud of this most unexpected work. This is all new territory for me. I thank you for the support.

Pretty Words. Nothing More.

With her kiss still fresh on his lips, he drove home. Lost in thought and replaying every moment from the perfect night, he could still taste her lip gloss, smell her perfume, and feel her breath meeting his.

His vision blurred when a few tears washed over his smiling eyes. As he nearly drove through a red light, he realized he didn't know if he was tearing up from the happiness of the evening or from the one lingering fear this may have been his only opportunity to enjoy her simple, precious kiss.

∞⟨Ɛ

I will earn your respect by offering you nothing less than my own.

I will earn your trust by giving you no reason to doubt me.

I will ease your fear by being brave enough for us both.

I will prove my worth by being worthy.

I have your friendship.
I am hopeful to gain your affection.

This is how I will earn it.
    This is how I will retain it.
        This is how I will value it.

Every day.

∞⟨Ɛ

Most men would notice her eventually.

He noticed her immediately.

ဢ၇ဢ

She did the absolute worst thing possible.
She didn't break his heart. In fact, she made it stronger.
She did, however refuse to accept it, and she was not kind
when doing so.

What she did was force this man, a once jaded, angry man,
turned tender and caring by her presence—she forced him
to truly look at her. She made him see her, not through
eyes dazzled by the veneer of affection, but through eyes
made for scrutiny.
Like a drill sergeant during inspection, he saw her every
flaw and realized he would have gone a lifetime without
noticing them, were it not for her harsh and abrupt refusal
to accept his heart.

He couldn't see her the same way anymore.
He didn't smile inside when she was near.
He knew her beauty hadn't changed.
He just missed feeling wonderful.

ဢ၇ဢ

He thought of places they would have seen
As the couple they should have been.

ဢ၇ဢ

She craved the darkness, but always asked the wrong man
to turn out the lights.

ဢ၇ဢ

He wanted to feel important and attractive to someone beautiful.

Even for a moment.
Even if it was all a lie.

These lies were so much less painful from the one he once thought worthy of his trust.

These were, for lack of a better term, honest lies.
These lies were worth the expense.

ℝ℞

It wasn't the allure of the night that kept him awake.

He knew if he made a fool-hearted attempt to sleep, he'd become a prisoner to his mind.
His own constantly moving and frequently dark thoughts would torment him, betray him, and cause him to feel even more pain.

Awake, he could hide behind his smile or a joke designed to fool those around him, to give the appearance of happy complacency.

Asleep, he would risk being trapped inside an evolving, unrelenting nightmare.

He would drink, carouse, and bark at the moon.
This was how he would exhaust his mind, in search of a few hours of painless slumber.

His mind, however, knew of his plan.

ℝ℞

Within mere moments, he knew he would love her.
They were perfectly matched in both kindness and in
darkness. She was damaged in the same ways.
Her eyes revealed hope and torment, and, much like him,
her stride suggested external confidence while it hid
internal awkwardness.

In short, she was the most beautiful thing he'd ever seen.

Acting upon pure instinct, he looked at her, and, without
even realizing what he was saying, told her,
"Our scars will match."

Startled, she looked at him, took a breath, and smiled.

₧₧

The bullet sped by his head with an eerie hiss and forced
its way into the wall behind him.
With bits of brick and the scent of gunpowder meeting his
startled face, fear and adrenaline caused his heart to race.

Looking back at the bullet hole, he breathed a sigh of
relief, which soon led to a steady flow of tears.

While happy he averted this tragedy, he became
increasingly disappointed for once again putting himself
into the line of fire.

His body froze into a deathly posture as he asked himself,
"How many near-misses do I have left?"

₧₧

It was her loss.
Yet, it was he who felt something was missing.

⊰⊱

As evenings went, this one was stellar.
With the bright lights of the city encouraging them to keep
the night alive, he brought her to a favorite place.
This bar was elegant and tacky all at once.
It suited the couple perfectly.
The moon was full, almost daring the man to steal another
kiss from her.
Still reeling from their first embrace, he resisted the
moon's challenge.
As they walked toward the entrance, she wrapped her arm
around his and gently allowed their hands to intertwine.
At that moment, they were together.
For that one brief instant, he felt whole.

⊰⊱

She was the object of his affection.
He was an object.
An affectation.

⊰⊱

He knew he would say "No" to her a thousand times
today.
He knew he would have said "Yes" as many times
yesterday.

He knew this was why he was foolish.
He knew this was why he was hurting.

⊰⊱

At first, he was haunted by her.
Time passed and healing occurred, but still, he felt her presence.
She was there. Watching from a distance.
She. Was. There.
She dismissed his advances and deemed his friendship unworthy of her.
She set up a private world where true friends and untrue lovers would entertain her, so long as everyone knew he was not allowed inside.
Was she monitoring his emotions, hoping he exhibited a proper amount of misery?
Perhaps, she missed him?
All he knew was…
She followed him.

ℰↃ℺

He would have given her the pain she desired.
She chose to be hurt in more conventional ways.

ℰↃ℺

She encouraged him.
She woke up this cynical, bitter man and returned music and light to him.
She brought out his smile.
She courted his passion.
She made him feel worthy of something grand.
And then,

She left.

She had other plans.

ℰↃ℺

His words meant nothing to her.
She was not moved by them.
She did not recognize them.
She did not trust them.
He wrote words of kindness and respect.

ᘓᘐ

Snapshots of the heavens, crazy desert skies.
He sent her tiny moments of the sun and moon's rise.
Today, there's only dust found on his camera's eye.
And no more reason for him to stop and share the sky.

ᘓᘐ

What I said to you
Was said only once
To only one.

ᘓᘐ

She dismissed his sincere, heartfelt words.
She would never witness his powerful, passionate affections.

ᘓᘐ

She threw him back after he was hooked.
Now, he won't take the bait.

ᘓᘐ

The music of her song enchanted him.
The madness of her mind imprisoned him.
The absence of her soul freed him.

ᘓᘐ

Ripples in the water intrigued her until curiosity drove her mad.
Casting her gaze onto the lake, she wondered what stirred the once calm water.
As the concentric circles of waves slowly crept outward, a vision quietly appeared.
Seeing only her reflection, she found her answer.
And she ran.
She believed herself to be a mythical beauty, with powers of wonder and charm.
She cast her spell on many.
She cast away the only one to fall.

ಬಂಃ

No one knew of the multifaceted stone within.
They only saw the craggy, soot-covered rock.

ಬಂಃ

The posture of the patient man was assumed by the man who was, somehow, always late to the party.

ಬಂಃ

The actions of many moved the pen of one.

She was not the first to break his heart.
She was not the only one to mislead him.
She was not unique when she let him down.
She was merely the most recent.

A sorrowful tale where she was one of many.

ಬಂಃ

Her frequent cries for help were subtle, and in close proximity.

By the time they heard his screams, he was well past the pain.

෨෬

He gave nothing away.
He'd not allow her familiar embrace to cause alarm.
It was a standard greeting, after all.
He remained calm in front of prying eyes.
He'd toil for pay and perform his tasks well.
Outward appearances presented an average day.
By design, it was a subtle gesture, a tiny caress signaling she was near.
The slightest graze of her fingertips across his back brought forth the widest of his smiles.
With her single, gentle touch he was elated.
His pure joy was evident to all.
He couldn't recall the last time he felt so exposed.
He hid nothing.

෨෬

As years passed, the bark wrapped itself around the jagged, rusty wire.

Stronger and taller she grew as the fence slowly came apart.

Living with the pain, she found beauty and majesty within her wounds.

෨෬

You need not carry forever, that tattered old rag.
Its frayed edges and hurtful stains hide more than time
past.

Your grip tightens as the memories return.
You cower under its familiar shroud.
Darkness clouds the sun above.

There is so much more waiting for you.

You need not throw away all those painful things.
Fold them neatly and keep them safe.
They are yours to guard, yours to share. Always.
Make tomorrow your daily companion.
Find comfort and warmth in the light of a brand new day.

☙❧

His heart knows he should
have listened better to
Night's perfect moon.

☙❧

Looking squarely at him with wonder and surprise,
A shade of green he'd never seen
And longing in her eyes.

☙❧

He exhibited remarkable strength and resolve around her.
And still, she made him weak.

☙❧

She vanished.
Why she remains hidden,
Why she left, are not for him to know.
She filled him to the brim with emotion and purpose.
With her absence, he was empty.
Without cause or reason,
She vanished.

⊱⊰

She can never take away the delight he gained from her
smile.

⊱⊰

To his detriment, she assumed his heart and mind would
always belong to another.

⊱⊰

To make her smile
To make her laugh
Was his pleasure.

To make her tremble
To make her shake
Was his honor.

To make her weep
To make her leave
Was his regret.

⊱⊰

The restraint he showed her was perfectly matched by
The restraints he owed her.

⊱⊰

She felt pain long before she felt the blade.

ℰℛ

He ran out of time to waste on chasing a dream.

ℰℛ

Only after salting the earth did she expect his love to grow.

ℰℛ

Tortured is the man whose
Siren **and M**use are one and the same.

ℰℛ

His fire cast shadows where his true self lived.

She was the first to see the hidden man inside.

He was the first to show her darkness.

They created heat, and new shadows danced in their light.

ℰℛ

His words were written on his heart.
She merely saw them.

Were they written on his chest,
She may have felt them.

ℰℛ

Everyone would tell her to love this man.
Sadly, she would listen to no one.

❧❧

A pretty envelope filled with pretty words.
A man's desperate heart emptied on the page.
Raw, handwritten emotion.
To chronicle such feelings was rare.
Rarer still, was for him to present them.
"All women dream of receiving such a gift," he was told.

Not so.

Validating his belief he was worthy of no one so beautiful,
She returned the pretty envelope filled with pretty words.

❧❧

Sun fire bursts of yellow propelled pinpoints of black
through him.
His armored soul was no match for her painful, passionate
stare.
A passing glance melted him.
A direct hit and he was lost forever to the girl and the
gunmetal blue of her eyes.

❧❧

He wanted every part of her to feel his warm breath on her
skin, and yearned to hear her heart beat loudly underneath
his.

❧❧

If it meant waiting until his dying breath, he would be the last man to kiss her well.

෨෬

With the starting line behind him, he was wise not to grow complacent.
He knew their journey would be long and troubled well before the finish line was in sight.
Only his belief in the destination's worth would compel him to make the trek.

෨෬

He was...

Her friend
  Her confidant
    Her advisor
      Her companion
      Her defender
       Her poet
      Her past
      Her present
    Her future
  Her admirer
Her fool.

He was not...

Hers.

෨෬

He learned being the right man was not enough.

෨෬

This was not the first time he had been misled by a
beautiful woman smiling under a brilliant moon.

✂✂

He had no idea he was winning.
He felt lost from the beginning.

✂✂

Every feature on her face
Every hair on her head
Every step in her stride
Every shadow from her shape
Brought him pure joy.

✂✂

She watched his smile slowly fade away.
She saw him disappear.
She knew he was a man filled with devotion.
She had forgotten he was a man with dignity.
She wondered if this was her doing.
She wondered if he would return.
She soon learned the answers, and then
She wept.

✂✂

It was long past time the man listened to a different song.

✂✂

In the blink of an eye,
It was a memory shared by two
And important to one.

✂✂

She kept him at arm's length while others had their way
Selfishly using his devotion against him.
Frustrated from watching lesser men claim her
Exhausted from waiting for her attention
He slipped away.
Missing comfort and hungry for respect, she looked for him.
The time had come for her to reach beyond her grasp.
An agile woman, with length of limb to touch the sky
She feared he may have traveled a length too far.

ဆာဌ

Crazed for attention, she craved the aftermath.
The little girl watched as the three boys fought.
Nibbling at her braid, a wicked grin and innocent eyes
emerged as she whispered to a fourth boy,

"Now, what is that all about?"

Selfish, destructive little girl.

ဆာဌ

Her only real power was transformation.
Becoming any one for any man.
Your fantasy in a flash.
Leading you on,
Encouraging you to believe in her.
A bewitching woman filled with lies.
The glamour faded, her true self revealed to him.
He could now discern between magic and charm.
She was a girl. Nothing more.
No witchcraft could enchant him.
No spell she cast would make him return.

ဆာဌ

He missed feeling something good about someone special.

A. Martello

ABOUT THE AUTHOR

Andy Martello is an award-winning author and freelance entertainer living in Las Vegas, Nevada. His first book, **The King of Casinos: Willie Martello and the El Rey Club**, has been sold in six different countries and earned ten literary awards, including an International Book Award and a USA Best Books Award for Best Biography.

When not writing, Andy makes frequent appearances on popular television programs such as **Mystery Diners** (Food Network), performs at comedy clubs and corporate events across the country, and he tours the U.S. and Canada as the announcer for **The Price is Right LIVE**, a live stage show version of TV's most famous game show.

This is Andy's second book and his first book of poetry.

Upcoming books include a deluxe limited edition of this work titled **Pretty Words. So Much More**, a second book of poetry titled **The Broken Mirror**, and the tentatively titled **And Here's Your Host... Insights and Interviews with Game Show Greats**.

www.andymartello.com

LIKE and FOLLOW Just A Martello Books
www.facebook.com/andymartelloentertainment

To donate to the Pretty Words Project, visit
www.gofundme.com/PrettyWordsProject

Pretty Words. Nothing More.

Andy Martello's award-winning book,
The King of Casinos:
Willie Martello and the El Rey Club is available at
Amazon, CreateSpace, and AndyMartello.com.